To my mum, dad and brother, who introduced me to a world full of love and laughter.

To my husband, who built a world with me and then filled it with joy.

To my little wild ones, who make the world brighter just for being here.

I love you.

hope

IS A

VERB

SIX STEPS TO RADICAL OPTIMISM WHEN THE WORLD SEEMS BROKEN

EMILY EHLERS

murdoch books

Sydney | London

contents

INTRODUCTION:
CHOOSING HOPE 6

Step one

STOP
FREAKING
OUT

12

Step two

CHANGE
THE STORY

54

Step three

SET YOUR
INNER
COMPASS

80

Step four

OWN YOUR
POWER

———

112

Step five

JUST
START

———

144

Step six

FIND YOUR
PEOPLE

———

176

FINAL THOUGHTS: WE'VE GOT THIS! 202

SUPPORT SERVICES 204 ✳ THANK YOU 206

INTRODUCTION

choosing
hope

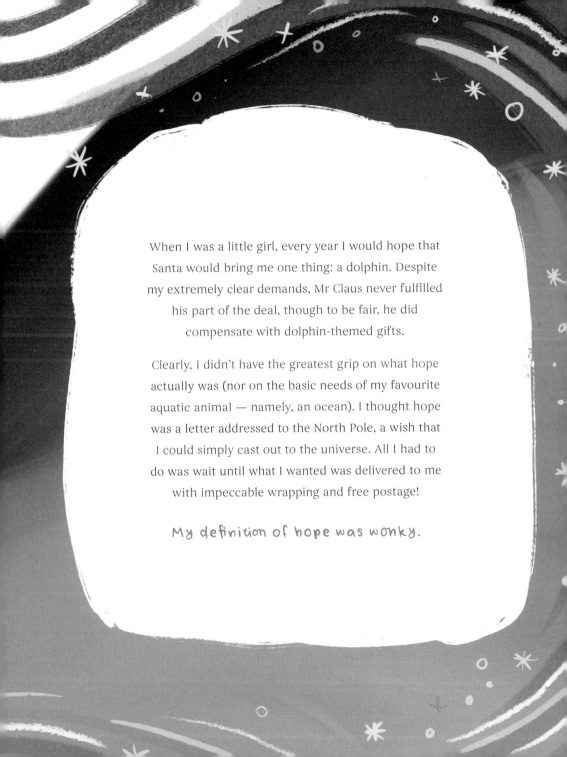

When I was a little girl, every year I would hope that Santa would bring me one thing: a dolphin. Despite my extremely clear demands, Mr Claus never fulfilled his part of the deal, though to be fair, he did compensate with dolphin-themed gifts.

Clearly, I didn't have the greatest grip on what hope actually was (nor on the basic needs of my favourite aquatic animal — namely, an ocean). I thought hope was a letter addressed to the North Pole, a wish that I could simply cast out to the universe. All I had to do was wait until what I wanted was delivered to me with impeccable wrapping and free postage!

My definition of hope was wonky.

What is hope?

In the broadest of terms, hope is a deep desire for something to happen. A quick scan of the official definitions explains that hope also comes with a side serving of expectation; while nothing is guaranteed, the core of hope is the simple belief that whatever we hope for *could* happen.

Studies indicate that when people have hope they are better able to manage stress, cope with setbacks, think creatively and achieve their goals. It is also an essential component for learning, motivation and improvement of skills. Hopeful people are often happier and more resilient, and even recover more quickly from physical ailments (possibly because they are highly motivated to participate in their healing).

Hope is essential for us to live our lives to their fullest potential.

But let's be honest, a quick glance around our planet can be enough to quickly dampen any warm, fuzzy feelings of hope. Climate change, pandemics, racism, poverty, extreme weather, economic uncertainty — the list goes on.

No wonder so many people are struggling with a sense that the sky is falling. No wonder so many of us are experiencing anxiety and even panic about the future. When times are hard, it's a hell of a lot easier to lose hope than it is to hold on to it. How can we feel hopeful when the world seems so ... hopeless?

Hope is a verb

Expecting to simply 'have' hope is a type of magical thinking that puts you at the mercy of your circumstances, as well as a million other precarious factors (such as: which headline did you happen to scroll past five minutes ago?). Waiting for hope is like waiting for a portly gentleman to drop a dolphin down your chimney; it's a wish, unlikely to come true.

But what if instead of waiting for hope to arrive, and in the meantime letting apathy and anxiety overwhelm us, we actively chose to be hopeful? What if we nurtured hope like a tiny flame, feeding it with new visions and inspiring possibilities, daily acts of kindness and courage, stronger communities and a deeper sense of purpose, until that flame started to glow on its own?

For hope to be meaningful, effective and empowering, it requires your participation. Hope isn't just something you have, it's something you do. Now, more than ever, we need individuals and communities to not only wish for change, but also to use it to light the way into the future.

This is active hope.
This is hope as a verb.

I have experienced hopelessness before (and likely will again) and have learned to follow certain steps whenever the world feels dark. These steps always help me keep the flame lit, even if it is only a flicker. And as I feel stronger, that flicker rekindles back into a flame.

This book provides a framework to help you find and nurture your own flame of hope and, in turn, a sense of radical optimism for the future. Crazy? Maybe. Worth trying? You'd better believe it. Because we're all in this together. And our future depends on our ability to not only hope for a better world, but also to make it possible.

We are all that we have, but my gosh we have a lot. Let's go.

author's Note

Unfortunately, this book is not maple syrup — it cannot
solve everything. We live in a world with very real systemic issues,
massive discrepancies in privilege, unpredictable laws of nature and
governments that sometimes impede human rights to satiate their
own desires. There are truly unfair things that happen in our world.

With that in mind, it is important to note that this book is not asking
you to do All The Things. It is about doing what you can; taking small,
simple steps that can help you nurture a sense of hope.

If you are struggling to cope in ways that are beyond the scope of this
book, please know that there are resources to help. Turn to page 204
for helplines, people and organisations that can assist you further.

stop FREAKING OUT

Bright eyed & bushy kaled!

A self-styled hippie (lotsa tie-dye)

Here's me, circa 2010.

*t*here I was, doing all the eco things. I'd quit plastic, was growing food, ran my own eco blog documenting my bona fide bohemian transformation.

And as the most recent development in Project Eco Warrior:

I HAD GONE VEGAN!

This change had followed an utter binge on documentaries about our global food system.

The more I learned, the guiltier I felt for having been complicit in these systems for so long.

HOW YOU RUINED THE ENTIRE WORLD

I started to feel like a small but not insignificant piece

in an increasingly complex puzzle.

Then one night I watched a documentary about
the overfishing of our oceans.

I couldn't get the images out of my head. Supertrawlers
prowling our beautiful oceans with gigantic nets scooping
up entire schools of fish. Rays and sharks caught up in the
melee. Fish left gasping on the decks. I would have
preferred to see Freddy Krueger in my dreams!

So, I did the sensible thing and decided that it was up to me
(and me alone) to save the entire world. Seemed feasible.

Let's just say, I was a DELIGHT to be around.

Put down the garlic prawn and read this pamphlet, you shrimp-murdering sociopath!

At that time, I was working long hours in a thankless corporate cubicle. My long commute consisted of mad dashes, crammed car parks and sweaty train rides. Every night, I arrived home after dark, exhausted — physically, mentally and spiritually.

At the end of one particularly long day, I was craving comfort, which we all know is a carbohydrate. I made a quick shopping list, but it was less ingredients and more rules.

Vegan
No Palm oil
Local
Plastic free
Ability to fix my entire life

As I walked the supermarket aisles, I became increasingly flummoxed. My loyal friend pasta was wrapped in plastic. The Hokkien noodles had travelled around the world to get to me. The corn chips were full of palm oil. Absolutely every carby comrade had something that I deemed dubious. Traitors.

It was at this precise moment of overwhelm that I found myself in the tuna aisle. It looked back at me like some kind of vegan-squashing supervillain.

This was only one aisle, in one store, in one suburb, in one country.

How many fish had been scooped up to make this many cans of tuna?

How many could possibly be left in the ocean?

I ran out of the store in floods of tears.

Something had broken inside of me.

I decided to order the 'worst burger ever' (according to that list, anyway).

I felt like a fraud.

And I quit. Everything.

Anxiety starts small, like pebbles thrown to get our attention. If you don't pay attention, those pebbles turn into rocks, and then to boulders. If you STILL don't react, you can be swept away in a landslide of apathy.

You've likely experienced this as well — being completely
overwhelmed by the enormity of an issue. Here: pick
a boulder to crush your hopes with.

So before we even begin, let's lighten the load
by getting rid of the easiest boulder first.

Good riddance! The last thing you need weighing you down
is the shame of not knowing, doing and being everything.

The problems we're facing are not fun. They are
full of pain that shows up as:

SADNESS

HOPELESSNESS

FEAR

ANGER & OUTRAGE

FRUSTRATION

EXHAUSTION

There is no denying that
it can be painful to be a living,
breathing, loving animal in a
world where things aren't always
just. Your pain is proof of
your beating heart.

An Emotional Pie Chart

- Good emotions
- Bad emotions
- Being human

It can be tempting to wish for a life without pain.

Most of us spend a large portion of our lives intentionally trying to avoid pain. It's why supermarket shelves are full of painkillers and numbing creams.

Sure, a life without pain would mean no broken hearts. No worrying about getting shots, stubbing your toe or waxing every inch of your body until you look like a dolphin (if you so wish).

However, a life without pain might not be so great. People born with the extremely rare condition known as Congenital Insensitivity to Pain (CIP) overwhelmingly report that a life without any pain sensation is more curse than blessing.

People with CIP often have shortened life spans. Their major symptoms are 'an accumulation of wounds', which happens for two reasons:

1. They lack physical feedback (pain) and therefore do not know to, say, move their hand off a hot stove.

2. They can become reckless because there seems to be no consequence. They feel infallible and push past their limitations.

Turns out pain is a vital component of survival.

While pain is important, it cannot be permanent.

Understanding what the world's problems are and why they are important is one thing: living alongside them, waiting for them to crush us at any moment, is quite another.

When we stop moving through these feelings and start living permanently in their shadow, our brains and bodies become more biologically conditioned to freak out: it becomes a pattern.

THIS   BECOMES   THAT

hurt ⟶ bitterness

sadness ⟿ depression

ANGER ⟶ bad temper

feAr ⟶ ANXIETY

guilt ⟶ shAme

Why does this happen?
Let's take a brief look at evolution
to understand why ...

A Very Brief Look

240 MILLION YEARS	200 MILLION YEARS
First dinosaurs (big lizards) appeared	First mammals appeared

If I were to boil the entirety of human evolution down into one sentence, it would be:

Lizards evolved into mammals, which then evolved into humans.

at Evolution

55 MILLION YEARS

First primate-like mammals appeared

200,000 teeny-tiny years

First Homo sapiens (us!) appeared

But I'm not a lizard anymore!

I hear you say, to which I reply,

Not really, but kind of ...

As we all know, you can tell the age of a tree by counting its rings. It's less well known that you can actually tell the story of its life — its growth, or evolution.

The first ring marks a year of growth. Happy birthday, tree!

The light wood indicates spring and summer growth.

Dark rings mark the colder months.

There is even, steady growth between the first few rings.

Little growth signifies a drought.

This dark scar shows that the tree survived a forest fire.

This dent tells the story of where a branch once lived.

Similarly, our brains tell the story of the whole process
of human evolution, from lizard to mammal to us.

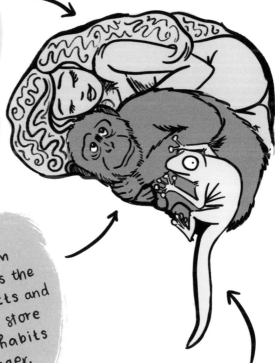

Our human brain
(the neocortex) is
the most advanced
part of the brain,
the rational home
of imagination,
abstract thought and
problem solving.

Our monkey brain
(the limbic system) is the
centre of our instincts and
emotions, where we store
memories, create habits
and predict danger.

Our lizard brain
(the stem and cerebellum)
is all about survival.
The slightest whiff
of danger and it hits
the panic button.

Each part of our brain serves an important purpose. Top item on the priority list? Stay alive.

Our brains are constantly surveying the horizon for danger (both consciously and subconsciously). If a threat is detected, we hit the panic button — a tiny hotbed of neurons called the amygdala.

The amygdala hijacks the rational prefrontal cortex and sends control straight down to our lizard brain. We go into survival mode with only three options: fight, flight or freeze.

If we are being chased by a bear, this is a good thing, triggering the perfect mix of hormones for us to hightail it out of there. Where this becomes a problem is when our amygdala is constantly firing. For example, when we become stuck in what I like to call

the Cycle of Doom.

The Cycle of Doom

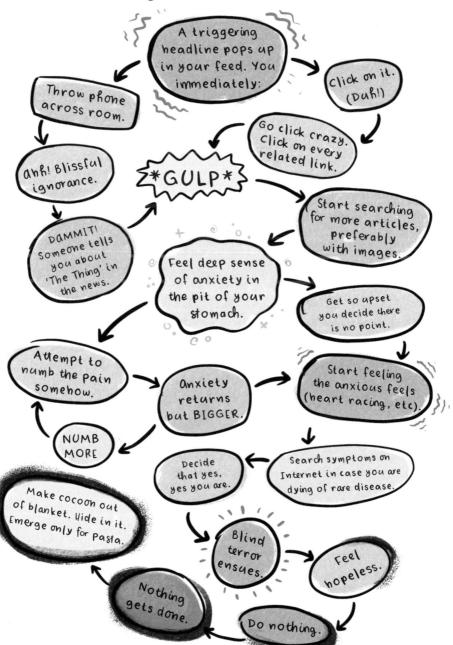

Sound familiar?
Your lizard brain doesn't know if there's an actual threat (for example, you poked a grizzly bear in the eye) or if you just read a statistic.

And it's not just your brain that is affected.

EGAD! A threat is perceived.

Your lizard brain sounds an alarm that triggers stress hormones to rush to your defence.

Cortisol! Adrenaline! GO!

Your body starts to react.

... temporarily shutting down your digestive system. (Hello dry mouth and stomach butterflies.)

What anxiety does to your body

Immediately, your breathing rate speeds up to make more oxygen in case you need to make like a cheetah and run.

... shutting off the sexy hormones. (You don't tend to feel super randy when faced with death!)

If you don't use that oxygen by running, it can make you feel light-headed & dizzy.

Your body diverts all energy possible to your muscles by ...

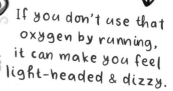

Your pupils dilate to let more light in (and make you better at spotting threats). Great for target practice but it can lead to blurred or tunnel vision, which adds to anxiety.

How Anxiety Feels

A belt around
the chest

A racing mind

Tingly
extremities

Inability to
concentrate

Extreme
restlessness

Dizziness

Jumpiness

Racing heart

Upset stomach

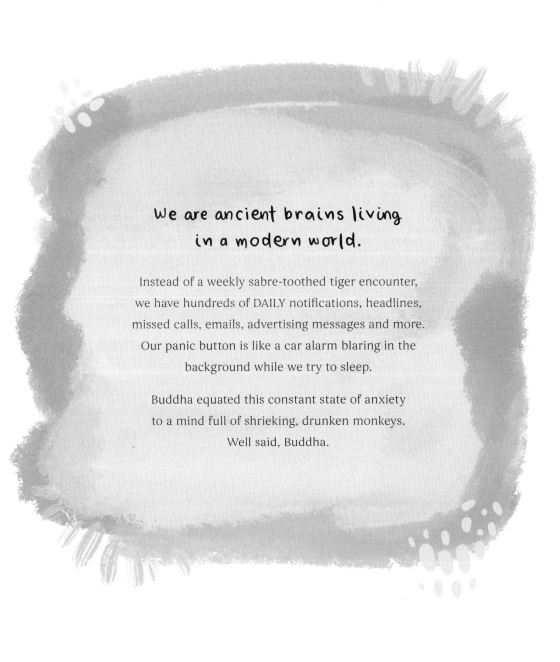

We are ancient brains living in a modern world.

Instead of a weekly sabre-toothed tiger encounter,
we have hundreds of DAILY notifications, headlines,
missed calls, emails, advertising messages and more.
Our panic button is like a car alarm blaring in the
background while we try to sleep.

Buddha equated this constant state of anxiety
to a mind full of shrieking, drunken monkeys.
Well said, Buddha.

Our collective anxiety is worth billions.
This is not a conspiracy theory, but a fact.

Fear of the way we look ...
keeps us spending.

Fear of not being successful ...
keeps us in a cycle of consumerism.

Fear of the 'other' ...
sways the way we vote.

Fear of being too loud, too much ...
keeps us small, quiet and manageable.

But let's not get stressed out about being stressed out. The more important question is:

What can we do about it?

When we allow our lizard brain to take
control, we limit our options to:

FIGHT
(rage & outrage)

FLIGHT
(quit, ignore & numb)

FREEZE
(anxiety & apathy)

In other words: FREAK OUT!

However, there is a fourth option.

Figure out!

When we keep our anxiety in check, we can stop our lizard brain from hijacking everything. This way — even though the world may seem scary — we can keep functioning and figuring out, rationally.

QUESTIONS TO ASK YOURSELF WHEN YOU'RE FREAKING OUT (instead of figuring out)

START

Am I in immediate danger (e.g. just aggressively tugged a tiger's tail)?

YES → Your panic is warranted. → Make like Joe Exotic and run!

NO → Remind yourself that you are safe. → Take 5 deep breaths. → Before you say 'but I feel really weird!' ...

You aren't crazy — you're freaking out. Your body is actually trying to help. But you are in control of the panic settings!

Identify what emotion you are feeling & say it out loud.

(This is called Emotional Recognition. The FBI even uses it to calm down tense situations!)

47

¡f?!

What if now is our time?

What if pain and anxiety are exactly the conditions we need to transform the way we've been doing things?

In his book *The Geography of Genius*, Eric Weiner notes that certain places, at certain times, have produced disproportionate bursts of geniuses. He calls them Genius Clusters.

Renaissance Florence produced Leonardo da Vinci, Michelangelo, Donatello and Botticelli. In 12th- and 13th-century Hangzhou, China, the world's first nautical and astronomical maps, fine textiles and porcelain, and even paper money were invented. Ancient Athens gave us Socrates, Plato and Aristotle.

In all these places where geniuses seemed to grow on trees, there were three conditions:

diversity,

discernment,

and

(*drum roll, please*)

disorder.

Geniuses are rarely born in times of peace.

We change and innovate when we have no other choice.

What if we are about to step into a golden era when everything changes?

Step two

change THE STORY

Our current collective attitude about the future is not one that makes us feel excited about heading there. But — unless we invent a time machine — we are moving forward whether we want to or not.

For individuals and our global community to feel energised, we need a new narrative about the possibilities of our planet and the people we share it with.

Let's imagine this journey to the future like a road trip. We all know the power of the person in control of the music. Your attitude is the soundtrack of your life. Choose well.

Does your attitude about the future need to change?

If we want
to cultivate hope
(in ourselves & others)
we need to understand
the art of attitude
change.

From a psychological viewpoint, our attitudes are
a set of emotions, beliefs and behaviours that we
have about, well, everything really.

OBJECTS

GROUPS

EVENTS

SYMBOLS

Our attitudes are just stories that we believe
to be true. We learn them from …

SOCIAL
CONDITIONING

LIFE EXPERIENCE

SOCIAL NORMS

OBSERVATION

The Attitude Cycle

the stories we hook onto

form our beliefs

which stir our feelings

which drive our actions

(which then reinforce)

NEVER DOUBT THE

Every culture (in the world and in history)
is based on story. Stories are written, sung,
lived, told, performed and learned.

They teach us about places we've never been,
and inspire us to go on our own adventures.

Stories shape our perspectives of the world.
They can start wars, or end them.
They can terrify, or inspire.

S.S. HATCHER

POWER OF STORIES

If we believe the wrong story it can keep us stuck. If we believe the right story it can move us forward.

The Danger of the Single Story

When we hear ONE story on repeat we start to believe it. But what if we are listening to the wrong story?

Chimamanda Ngozi Adichie spoke of 'the danger of the single story' in her sensational TED Talk of the same name. Now a bestselling author, she remembered growing up as an avid reader in Nigeria. All the books she read were British or American and featured people with white skin and blue eyes who ate apples and drank ginger beer.

Entranced by storytelling, she started to write her own stories. Her stories featured people with white skin and blue eyes who ate apples and drank ginger beer. This, despite the fact that she was a girl with skin the colour of chocolate who ate mangoes and didn't even know what ginger beer was.

The point is that she didn't know people like her could exist in literature.

Single stories rob us of possibilities. They narrow our world view.

When we intentionally choose to create new stories (in our lives and the world), we open ourselves up to new possibilities and maybe new endings.

We are the plot twists the world has been waiting for.

Humans NEED stories.

They give us meaning, and meaning
is what keeps us moving forward.
It is not a 'bad attitude' that leads
to apathy, it is simply the lack of a
good story to keep us engaged.
That's what keeps us going,
even when we're tired.

Does that story serve you?

Plot yourself along the scales below.

DESPAIR   HOPE
_____

EXHAUSTED   ENERGISED
_____

If you're leaning to the left, it's likely you have a negative prognosis of the future. This is where you need to reframe your story; look at it in a different way.

(This is not to say feelings of exhaustion or despair aren't valid, but if that's the only track your mind is playing, it will burn you out. We don't need martyrs, we need you.)

Give your narrator a pep talk!

Your inner voice is the narrator of your life story. If it keeps pointing out everything that's wrong with the world, that's all you will see. But what if your narrator took a different approach? Here are a few questions to help you reframe your story about the future:

Could this be a new beginning?

What could the future look like (the future you want)?

List three people you see doing good in the world.

List three things that give you hope.

List three positive things that you could do to help.

Rethink your genre

Philosophers have long said that one of the most important decisions each of us makes is whether we believe we live in a hostile or friendly universe. Are you narrating your life as a comedy, or a tragedy? If you could pick a new genre for your story, what would it be?

HORROR

COMEDY

ADVENTURE

ACTION

TRAGEDY

FEEL GOOD

Your Hero's Journey

In 1949, Joseph Campbell saw that there was one story structure that showed up over and over: the hero's journey.

Meet our hero: a normal person living in an ordinary world.

A disruption occurs and our hero realises that there is disharmony in the world.

She tries to ignore the problem — because rising to the challenge takes courage!

But adventure keeps calling. Our hero rises and takes

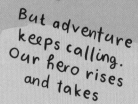

A LEAP OF FAITH

Embrace plot twists

As the hero's journey reminds us, life is not linear.
When challenges arise (as they do in every good story),
they might feel insurmountable.

But if we stay focused on the bigger picture, we can accept
that challenges are just part of the journey.

When we face a barrier, we can choose to stay stuck

or we can look for the light and do whatever we can to keep moving towards it.

REFRAME YOUR LANGUAGE

The words we use are important. We can carefully select our language to ignite fear or inspire hope, to divide or unite.

Often, changemakers and motivators use military or sporting terms. You know, the strong beats the weak, the winners beat the losers, good conquers evil.

This thinking relies on polarity: black versus white. But the truth is grey. If we use language that reinforces that there are winners and losers, there will always be conflict.

When our language is about destruction, we focus on what we'll destroy. But when our language is about creation, we focus on what we'll build. Not only is this more inspiring, it is also more instructive.

Conflict can start a riot. Inspiration can start a revolution.

Instead of this	Say that
Let's FIGHT that	Let's CHANGE this
DESTROY the old	BUILD the new
We should ABOLISH that	Let's REIMAGINE this
I CAN'T do that	I can't do this YET
We're DOOMED	We're LEARNING
Everything is BROKEN	What is this here to TEACH me?

Change your story
and you change
your life.

Change your life
and you change
the world.

Step three

SET YOUR
inner
COMPASS

Knowing the story that you want to create is one thing. Sticking the course is quite another.

Living a values-led life in the great wild world can feel like you're constantly paddling upstream. Sometimes it is ever so tempting to just let the current of conformity sweep you up and drift off in the same direction as the rest of the crowd.

When you do that, though, you might get the uncomfortable feeling of going against who it is you really are. Sure, it's easy, but it doesn't feel right. This is the feeling of acting out of line with your beliefs, of being out of alignment with your true self.

Going with YOUR flow might take courage and effort, but you will be an active participant in your own life. You will be fuelled by passion and purpose, two of the most important ingredients in nurturing hope.

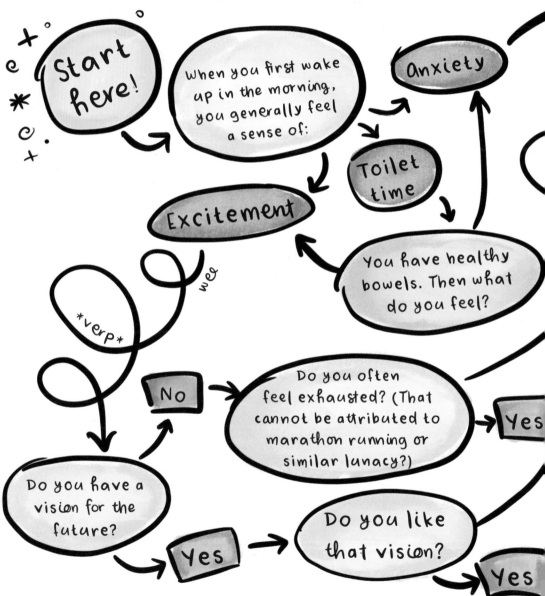

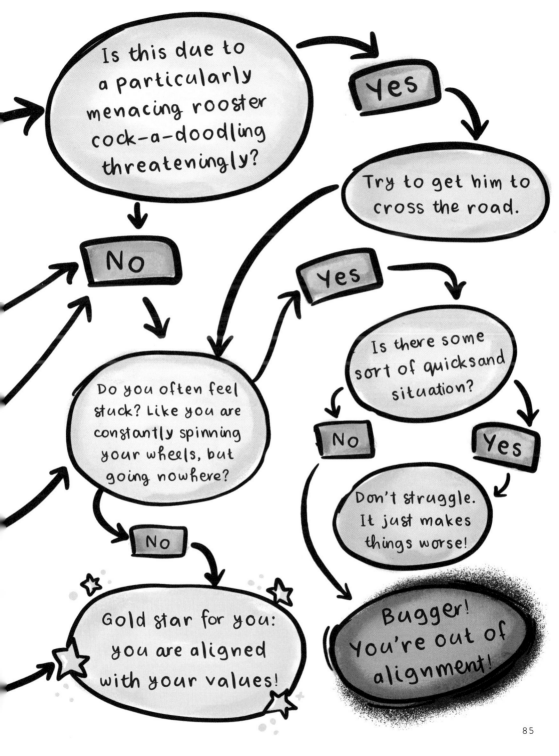

When we find ourselves out of alignment,
we feel it in every part of our body.

It's the twinge of feeling inauthentic, like a fraud,
like we're trying to fit in but we don't.

It's our heart, our head and our gut coming together to tell
us, *it might be easier this way, but it doesn't feel right.*

This is our inner compass — our true north — letting us
know that we are way off course. We are heading in a
direction that is not in line with our values.

It's easy to go
with the strongest
current, but it
might take you in
the wrong direction.
Follow your heart.
Stay on course.

This is PAINFUL

This iS SATISFACTION

So, I heard the other day that you should be able to name your five most important values off the top of your head. Could you?

Yeah, easy! Family, friends, health...

No, no, no! Those are WAY too broad. It's like how in beauty competitions they all say 'world peace'!

But then doesn't that mean we all have the same values?

Kinda, but no. If you look at
Abraham Maslow's Hierarchy of
Needs, you see that we humans all
share three basic psychological needs.

We all need:

To feel safe.

To feel that we belong.

To feel that we matter,
    that we're significant.

But behind those
three points, there is
an ocean of possibility
for how we live
our lives.

And our values guide the way!

Exactly!

adventure   growth   risk   challenge

belonging   community   closeness

satisfaction   joy   contentment   comfort

connection   spirituality   self-actualisation

independence   freedom   creativity   sovereignty

wisdom   knowledge   education   mastery

How to find your true north

 Point directly up.

 Figure out what matters most to you (psst: your values).

 Start to unlearn what you've been told you SHOULD value.

 Pay attention to the behaviours, habits and people that don't feel true to you and just let them go.

 Take notice of the behaviours, habits and people that light you up and celebrate them!

Reasons to value your values

They are
YOU-nique.

They change
with you

but can only be
changed by you.

They are helpful
decision-makers.

It feels good to
follow them

(unless you
value farts).

They aren't always
easy to follow,
but it's harder
when you don't.

Even when you
lose them, they
guide you
back to them
in whispers.

They fill
your life with
purpose and
direction.

There's a recurring plotline that we see
popping up a lot in our busy world.

Your values are those ever-present landmarks that (if you follow them) will deliver your best, most useful self to the world.

A difficult hike but has a beautiful view from the top

The foothills of Beliefs

The Forest of Feelings

Habit Hill

The Great Lake of Choices

Behaviour Bay

Can be scary!

The Cave of Apathy

The Bog of Judgement
(very smelly here)

The Rapids of Change

Fear Falls

The Stream of Skills

Disillusionment Desert

The Pit of Self-doubt

The Fertile Grounds of Action

The Lagoon of Strength

The Shores of Self-esteem
(prone to erosion)

The Delta of Identity

The Hidden Inlet of Potential

The wild, wide, wonderful ocean where we connect to the rest of the world

So let's take a deep dive and figure out what you treasure most in your life.

Start a JOY journal

 Choose a period of time, between two and seven days, making sure to include both a workday* and a day when you don't work.

 Be observant. Start to notice:

 When you feel moments of BLISS. This is when you lose track of time, your energy is high and you feel buzzed afterwards.

 When you feel moments of MEH. This is when time draaaags, your energy ebbs and you end up feeling drained.

 Write them down.

 Look for the commonalities in both categories. What makes you feel blissful? Do more of that. What makes you meh-ful? Do less of that.

* 'work' includes work within the home as a carer. Just because it's unpaid doesn't mean it ain't work!

Your more-or-less list

⭐ In your Joy Journal, make two columns, one titled LESS and one titled MORE.

⭐ Look at your journal and start filling it in. Every time you fill in one column, write the opposing option in the other.

LESS	MORE
buying	giving
scrolling	learning
gossiping	listening
self-loathing	action
fear	meditation
complaining	helping
suffering	asking
loneliness	connection

Now, let's go back to the start, before the world told you how you should be.

Back to your inner child.

Reasons why kids are awesome

(or, why you need to reconnect with your inner child)

They have a strong sense of justice

They unabashedly fly their freak flag

They choose wonder

They play all the time

They have bucketloads of empathy

They don't logic themselves out of trying, or dreaming big

There's another thing that children are MARVELLOUSLY talented at.

And that thing is —

wait, actually, first:

WHAT'S THIS?

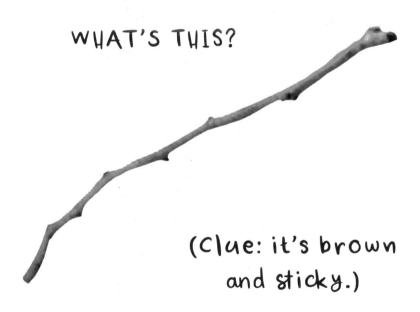

(Clue: it's brown and sticky.)

Most people see a stick. That's because we have been blunted by adulthood. We have lost the art of lateral thinking.

Where we see a stick, a child sees ...

a valuable building material

a wand

a fishing rod

a dancing cane

a conductor's baton

a paintbrush

We desperately need to re-engage with our ability
to think bigger, better and more bonkers.

Maybe then, instead
of seeing a mountain
of a problem,

A big problem

we would see a bunch of opportunities.

A mountain
to climb

A new place
to discover

A new dream
to be dreamed

A hurdle
to jump

An invention
to invent

An opportunity
to help

Questions to reawaken your inner child

When people reminisce about the 'child you', what themes and phrases keep coming up?

As a kid, what did you love doing most? What activities did you lose yourself in?

What were you good at? (P.S. This is in YOUR opinion. Ignore any past confidence-smashing comments!)

Was there a world event that profoundly impacted you in childhood? Why do you think it had that effect?

As a child, who were the people you looked up to the most (famous or not)? What was it that you admired about them?

People

Documentaries

Podcasts

Books

Find clues from your favourite things

Quotes or sayings

Movies

Speeches (TED Talks, historic speeches, commencement addresses)

Literary characters

Clarity-creating questions

What are you GOOD at?

What do you enjoy doing?

Because we can't always trust our own self-esteem, ask five friends to describe you in three words.

What world issues stick with you the most (the stories that sneak up on you at 3 am)?

How could you use your skills and strengths to help the issues that resonate most strongly with you?

How could you add joy to your life, and thus to the world?

When you live in alignment with your
values, you are your best self.

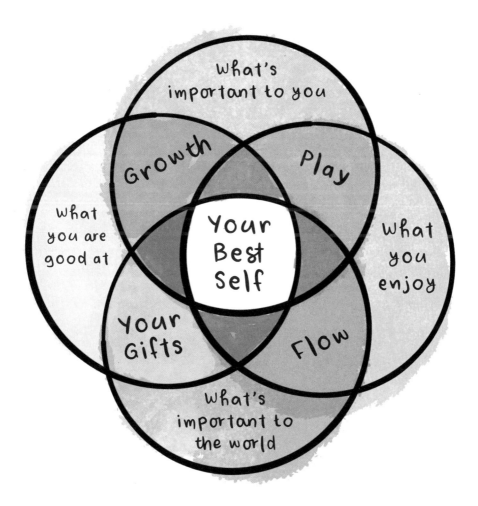

And the world is so very much in need of your radiant bestness!

Can values be bad?

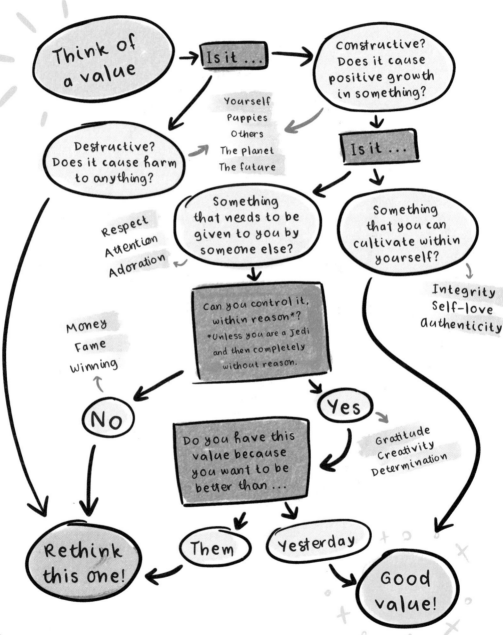

Think of a value

Is it ...

Constructive? Does it cause positive growth in something?

Destructive? Does it cause harm to anything?

Yourself
Puppies
Others
The planet
The future

Is it ...

Something that needs to be given to you by someone else?

Something that you can cultivate within yourself?

Respect
Attention
Adoration

Can you control it, within reason*? *Unless you are a Jedi and then completely without reason.

Integrity
Self-love
Authenticity

Money
Fame
Winning

No

Yes

Gratitude
Creativity
Determination

Do you have this value because you want to be better than ...

Rethink this one!

Them

Yesterday

Good value!

Now look back at everything you have written and identify three to five values. Write them down and put them somewhere you will see them regularly.

creativity PRESENCE Passion FREEDOM

poise silliness INTEGRITY humour

SCIENCE adventure JOY duty

hospitality JUSTICE generosity PIETY

fitness WISDOM perseverance MASTERY

love delight EQUALITY intrepidity

SELF-RESPECT fun spirituality

ambition grace INFLUENCE discipline

ZEAL NATURE faith inclusivity

order generosity DISCOVERY

PRIVaCY knowledge logic

fairness RESILIENCE reliability

learning RESOURCeFULNESS ingenuity

meaning DESIRE ease moxie

WONDeR independence spunk

ENVIRONMENTALISM growth ART

integrity SeRVICe truth

security devotion SEXUALITY

Wear your values proudly for the world to see.

Step four

OWN YOUR POWER

As meaning-seeking humans living on a small planet in an endless universe, it's easy to feel irrelevant. How can one person make a difference? Does what we do even matter?

Whenever I feel like I'm floating too far off into space, I grab onto the anchor of all the ways that I am connected. That everything is connected.

We are all interconnected, parts of the same ecosystem.

'Systems thinking' is the idea that the strength of an individual species is determined by the strength of the ecosystem it is part of. And each small part needs to thrive for the larger whole to function.

The whole is so much more than the sum of its parts.

You may be small, but you are vital.

An ecosystem needs every living thing, no matter how small. Microscopic bacteria nourish the plants, which feed the herbivores, and so on. Though the crocodile or the cassowary may look the mightiest, they are still dependent on the worms in the ground.

Our communities are also ecosystems,
dependent on each of us as well as on each other.

We all matter!

An old proverb says that if you think you are too small to make a difference, try sleeping in a room with a mosquito!

One way that we can each positively impact the world
is with kindness. Kindness buoys and energises us.
It restores resilience in the helpers of the world.
Take a moment to think of a few instances when
a simple act of kindness impacted your life.

The one who
welcomed you

The one who
showed up

The one who
believed in you

The one who
took the time

The one who
stopped to help

The one who
listened

How to own your power

One of the key principles of Stoicism, an ancient philosophy,
is that we must accept the things we cannot control and
instead focus on what we can.

If you focus on all the things you can't control (like the laws of nature), you can become overwhelmed, shrink yourself and withdraw. It's hard to have a positive impact in this place.

When you focus on what you CAN control, the way forward becomes clear. You can start taking action, leading the way for others. You become powerful!

A story about Scope of Influence

Once upon a time, a young man in the city dreamed of the wilderness.
In reality, he just had a patch of dirt.

Then one day, he decided to grow his own wilderness.

Bit by bit he learned and bit by bit it grew.

The plants started attracting wildlife to his yard ...

as well as compliments from his neighbours.

Soon, his neighbours began growing their own gardens. They started swapping advice ...

and clippings, compost, tips, tricks and spoils!

He doesn't dream of the wilderness anymore. And he lived happily ever after.

By controlling these things ...

How we treat others
How we vote
How we use our voices
How we show up for others
How we spend our dollars
The companies we support
Our habits, mindsets and attitudes
The messages we consume
The knowledge we seek out
The language we use

we influence these things!

The energy of others

The leaders in power

The systems we build
(or pull down)

The culture of our
communities

The lives of future
generations

How we feel about
the future

BREAKFAST: A Case Study

Let's look at how one small part of your day impacts
the world. Tomorrow morning, look at your breakfast
and ask yourself three questions*.

*This list of questions is non-exhaustive, and everyone
has their own circumstances that may limit options;
however, it is an example of questions we CAN ask.*

WHERE did it come from?

Was it imported, creating large travel emissions?

Or local, thus seasonal, healthier and supporting your local economy?

WHO did it come from?

Were the workers treated well and paid fairly?

Were the animals treated humanely?

HOW did it come?

Was it packaged in a wasteful way?

Is there a lower waste option you could explore?

Hope is a verb.
It's a doing word.
'Doing' requires energy
and resilience.
Therefore, to stay
hopeful you need to
look after yourself.

Sustainability is all about how we balance our needs with the needs of others and the future.

The art of sustainability is often represented by a three-legged stool. Each leg represents one of the three pillars of society (economy, environment and social equity).

ECONOMY

SOCIAL EQUITY

ENVIRONMENT

If one leg is ignored, is shorter or breaks, balance is destroyed. The planet cannot function healthily.

It's the same with us. There are three pillars of a person: mind, body and soul. We need all three to stay strong.

Just like with the planet, we need to balance what we take out with what we put back in. It's critical to prioritise wellness so we have the energy to stay hopeful and do good in the world.

Otherwise →

Let's take a quick look at your stool (not like that!)

Rate how satisfied you are in these pillars of your life:

Make a ritual of using this tool to quickly appraise
your wellbeing and identify what self-care needs
you have at any given moment.

call a friend or professional

Go people-watching

Journal your thoughts

Learn a new skill

LOOK after your MIND

EXERCISE

WATCH SOMETHING INSPIRING

MEDITATE

Spend time with someone you love

THE TOXIC TIMES
DOOM + GLOOM
SAD

Schedule time off social media and the news (at least set time limits)

Drink water
(boring but
true!)

walk

Eat lots of
plants

Prioritise
sleep

and
rest

STRETCH

Look after
your
BODY

Move your body
(in a way you love)

Track your
cycles: mood,
menstrual,
energy or all
of the above

Spend
time in
nature

Let your skin
touch the earth

Find awe daily

Make a habit of noticing beauty

PLAY!

DANCE

Look after your SOUL

Add rituals to your day

Pray

Cuddle an animal

Discover new places (get lost!)

Listen to or play music

How to Stay Well
KNOW. YOUR. SIGNS.

Burning out rarely happens overnight. Start noticing the
behaviours that signal you need to up your self-care.
Everyone is different, but here are some examples.

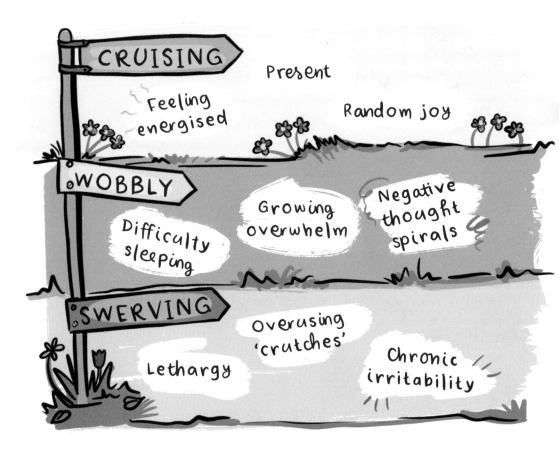

CRUISING

Present

Feeling energised

Random joy

WOBBLY

Growing overwhelm

Negative thought spirals

Difficulty sleeping

SWERVING

Overusing 'crutches'

Chronic irritability

Lethargy

Pay attention to avoid crashing.

THE GRATITUDE ATTITUDE

One powerful, energising habit that is available to us all is a GRATITUDE ritual.
Take a moment, at least once a day, to acknowledge three things you are grateful for.

A gratitude ritual isn't there to remind you of everything you have; it's reminding you to look for it!

NURTURE RESILIENCE

Leader bird

Our journey towards a better future isn't some short skip across the pond; it's a long-haul flight.

We need to carefully nurture our resilience to make sure we don't burn out. We also need to keep an eye on those flying with us, especially our most vulnerable.

We need to be like wild geese migrating together.

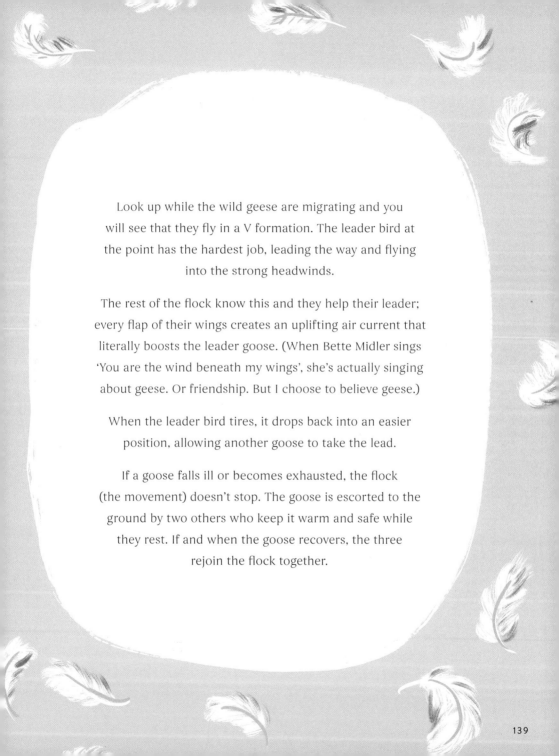

Look up while the wild geese are migrating and you will see that they fly in a V formation. The leader bird at the point has the hardest job, leading the way and flying into the strong headwinds.

The rest of the flock know this and they help their leader; every flap of their wings creates an uplifting air current that literally boosts the leader goose. (When Bette Midler sings 'You are the wind beneath my wings', she's actually singing about geese. Or friendship. But I choose to believe geese.)

When the leader bird tires, it drops back into an easier position, allowing another goose to take the lead.

If a goose falls ill or becomes exhausted, the flock (the movement) doesn't stop. The goose is escorted to the ground by two others who keep it warm and safe while they rest. If and when the goose recovers, the three rejoin the flock together.

Stay mindful of your energy
and that of those flying
alongside you.

Check your goose energy.

Check their goose energy.

Respect both.

What's Your Goose Energy?

Leader Goose

You are full of energy
and ready to lead.

Fall-behind Goose

You've been leading for a
while and need to ease back
for a bit.

Exhausted Goose

You need to rest
and be cared for.

Flock Goose

You're part of the
movement, lifting others
as you go.

With every day,
with every choice,
you impact
the world in
countless ways ...

how
wonderful!

Step five

just START

Hope is not about closing your eyes to the world's wicked problems and wishing they would disappear. It's about imagining a brighter future and then taking steps, no matter how small, to make that vision a reality.

*Y*ou can't do everything. No-one can do that. But you can do something.

Once you're ready to be helpful, it's time to get clear on what you want to positively impact.

This doesn't mean you choose only one cause to care about and ignore the rest, as in 'Save the children but damn the polar bears!' No. It's just about choosing one cause, right now. It's simply a starting point to channel your energy, stoked by curiosity and compassion.

As you continue along the path of being a force for hope and good in the world, your curiosity will take you on all sorts of twists and turns. You don't need to know exactly where you'll end up, you just need to start.

where to start

Help comes in all different shapes, sizes and styles.
It just requires action! Which action archetype(s)
do you see yourself in?

The Healer

The Joy-giver

The Fundraiser

The Picker-upper

The Helper

The Mentor

The Scientist

The Example

The Organiser

The Activist

The Doer

The Engineer

The Teacher

The Spirit-lifter

The Artist

The Conscious
Business Owner

The Pundit

The Designer

The Speaker-upper

The Number
Cruncher

The Participator

Every one of us has something unique and brilliant to offer the world — if we're brave enough!

Wondering how to find your voice?
What are your . . .

talents

your voice

passions

ideas

Take action

Kindness

VOICE

Use your Platform

Call people out
&
Call people in

VOTE!

Design

Create

Heal

SKILLS

Help

Calculate

Engineer

Repurpose

Compost

WASTE & STUFF

Donate

Choose less & ethically

(look up share compost programs in your area if you don't have room)

with your ...

Volunteer

Give Companionship

Animal shelters

Aged care homes

Foster programs

Teach a skill

TIME

Learn a skill

Lend a hand

Babysitting

Become a mentor

errands for someone less able

Fundraise

MONEY

Spend consciously

Support local small businesses — consider people & planet

Donate

What you can

A % of your income or profit

Invest in organisations doing good

You don't have to do everything at once. Pick one thing.

All great things start off small.

Just ask an acorn.

How to succeed at anything (everything, actually)

Try → Make mistakes → Giggle sheepishly → Learn → Try again → Learn more → Try

Still unsure where to start?

Look at the BIG picture.

Now zoom in.

Zoom in again.

And again.

Start here

How it feels when we're asked to change the world.

vs.

How it feels when we're asked to change our communities.

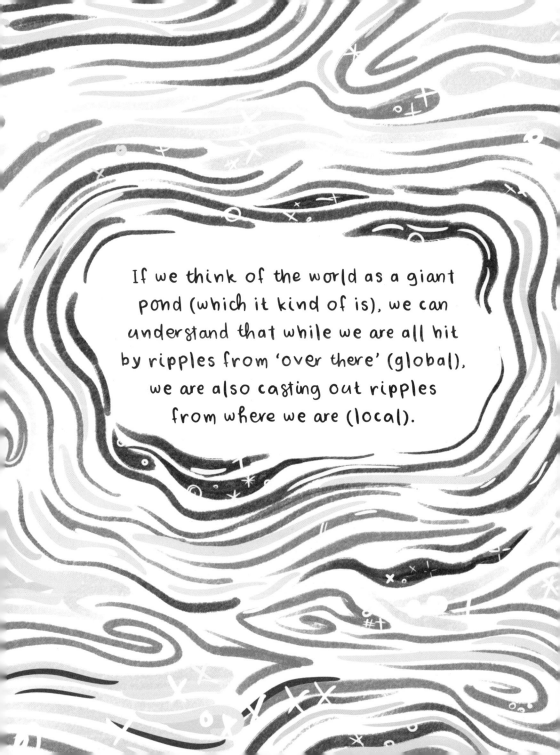

If we think of the world as a giant pond (which it kind of is), we can understand that while we are all hit by ripples from 'over there' (global), we are also casting out ripples from where we are (local).

Be a local legend!

Set up local projects such as a street library or community garden.

Support local businesses. Introduce yourself. Remember their names.

If you have excess fruit, don't let it rot on the ground; offer it to passers-by.

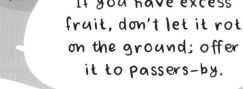

Volunteer!

How to be helpful

1. See problem
2. Be ~~superhero~~ human
3. Help

In Australia, bushfires are and always have been a fact of life. However, the 2019-20 fire season made a particularly early debut when a number of fires started in October. They were worrying (as always), but didn't seem too far from the ordinary. Then they kept getting bigger. By January, the world was watching in horror as apocalyptic images unfolded.

As an Australian (albeit one on the west coast, far from the literal line of fire), I can say that the atmosphere was a mixture of apprehension, anxiety and mourning. On the east coast, cities were swathed in thick smoke, like the set of some dystopian movie.

It was quite literally a David and Goliath moment. The fire power had stretched beyond what human power could match, let alone quench. It felt utterly hopeless.

Then, something happened.

People started doing what they could.

Anything they could.

Elderly volunteers handed out care packages.

People from all around the world donated money to people, places & animals.

Collage of

Musicians held concerts to raise funds.

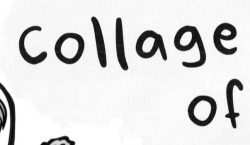

People gave their laundry baskets & time to nurse injured koalas back to health.

People without homes were offered a bed & a meal by a Sudanese refugee & his girlfriend. They all made a home concert using spoons for instruments & a torch for the 'lighting equipment'.

Artists & photographers sold their work to raise funds.

Childcare centres provided free child care to people who had lost homes or who were helping with the fire.

Sikh volunteers cooked food for those impacted by the fires.

the

Farmers offered their land for the livestock of other farmers who had damaged properties.

helpers

Comedian Celeste Barber used her platform to raise over 50 million dollars!

Knitters made pouches for healing animals.

People all over the country organised drives to replace food, clothing, toys & furniture for those in need.

Of course, kindness didn't quench the fires (the rains, mercifully, assisted the firefighters in doing that), but it unified and energised the communities.

On politics

It's ironic that when it comes to individual action,
one of the most important things you can do is collective.
I am, of course, talking about voting — or, as my 16-year-old
self would have said, 'Ugh, politics.'

Ah, sweet teenage me, sitting comfortably in my privilege
and my rainbow Doc Martens. I don't blame myself for not
being interested in politics then. I had no idea that my
simple existence was political. I also didn't understand
that my right to vote (when I turned 18, at least) was
one that women had fought hard for, a right still
denied to many women today.

I also thought that I had to know everything to have a say in
anything. I have a sneaking suspicion that many adults think
this way, too. How many times have you heard (or said),
'Oh no, I'm just not really a political person', in order to bow
out of conversations, uttering words of disengagement?

However, in a world where bad policies are made and
good policies are missing, we all need to treat this
right a little more like a duty.

Are you a political person?

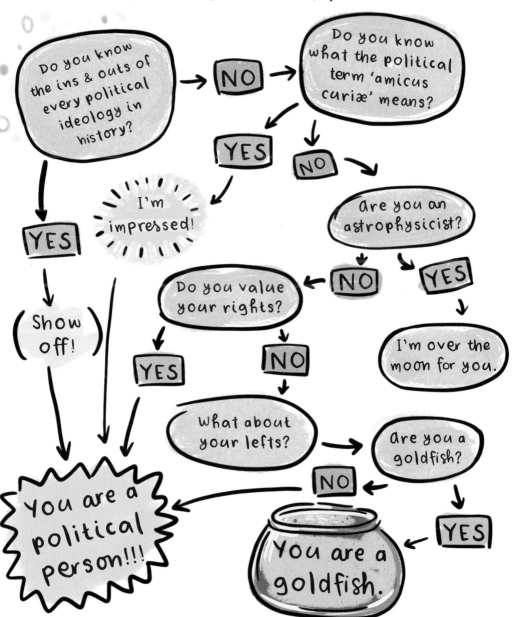

PSa. You do
not need to be
perfect to make
a difference in
the world.

Imperfect people making a difference

The person who is vegan
but ever so occasionally
eats cheese

The person new to allyship
who used the wrong pronoun
and is learning from it

The person who reduced her
plastic waste but is still
learning about food waste

The person who made
a mistake but is trying

The person who is learning
to think in a new way

The person who loves the planet
but has to fly for her work

The wild ride

Going about your normal life (basically, you're a tad oblivious to a few things).

You learn about an issue.

Guilt Canyon

'OMG, I'm going to vomit!'

Back to the start, where you get to choose how you'll make the people about to get on the ride feel: scared or excited?

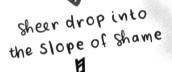

Sheer drop into the slope of shame

'Why didn't I know better?!'

# of habit change

Fundamental Peak
Lots of screaming and waving arms in the air as you yell at everyone to get on your page!

A Steep Learning Curve

The Full Circle of Empathy

That magical moment when you realise that no-one is perfect — not even you — and that's okay!

Fill in this letter to yourself

Dear Me,

I'm an absolute legend for choosing to be the change I wish to see, and I just got more clarity on what that is.

I have chosen (as a start) to focus my energy on _____
_____ because I want to live in a world where
_____
_____.

and I believe in _____
I am passionate about _____
and want to help _____.
by _____

My BIG dream is to change the world by _____;
_____
an awesome goal, if you ask me. But I know it will take time and consistent action so I'm not going to burn myself out by trying to do it all in one day.

Instead, I will start by doing what I can. _____,
I can _____,
and _____.
and _____.

I commit to _____
I will know I have reached this goal when _____
_____
and then I will start again with another goal.

This is how I will change the world. It's how people always have.

Love always, Me
P.S. You still owe me fifty bucks.

MYTH

Motivation

↳ leads to ↘

action

TRUTH

action

↳ leads to ↘

motivation

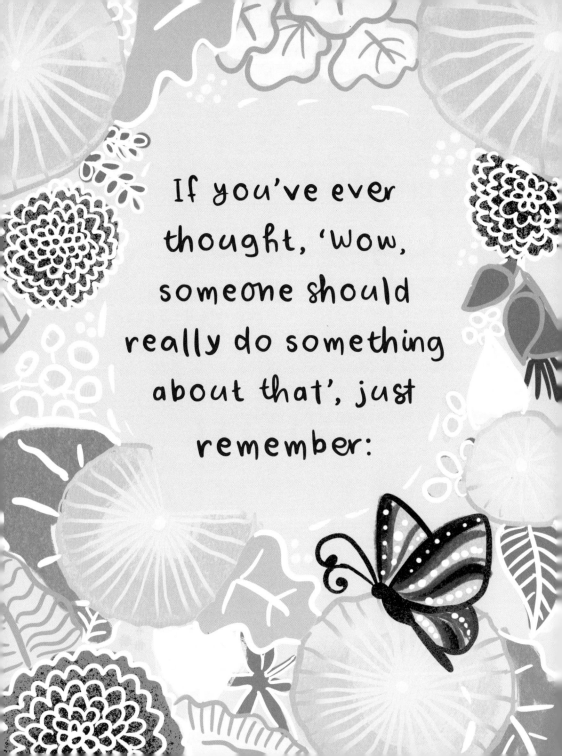

If you've ever thought, 'Wow, someone should really do something about that', just remember:

You're someone!

Step six

There are many animals that live on their own without a community: snow leopards, bears, the Tassie devil. Humans ain't one of those species. Along with cats and naked mole rats, we are social animals. We need our kin, our tribe, our social groups.

Social groups aren't just good for our souls (though they are); they are essential for our physical, emotional and spiritual wellbeing. This has roots in our biology and evolution. Back in the Palaeolithic era, a single human separated from their tribe was no match for the wild. Nowadays it's no different (though there are fewer sabre-toothed tigers to worry about).

Our greatest strength is — and always has been — our community.

With the advent of technology and social media, and the rise of individualism, it can be easy to feel like we can make it on our own.

SPOILER ALERT: we can't.

Do you need community?

A 'community' is simply a group of people tied together by a common unity. The group can be large or small, digital or in person.

We can survive without digital communities, but we cannot survive without actual human contact. It is vital to a long, healthy life.

Communities can be formed through connections of

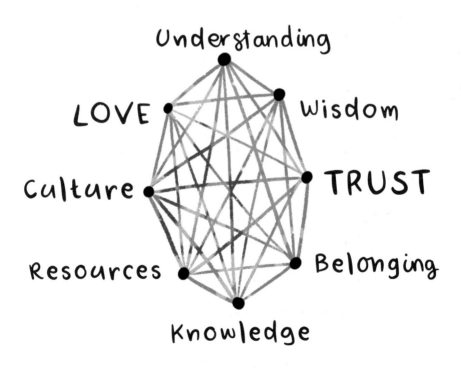

Understanding

LOVE   Wisdom

Culture   TRUST

Resources   Belonging

Knowledge

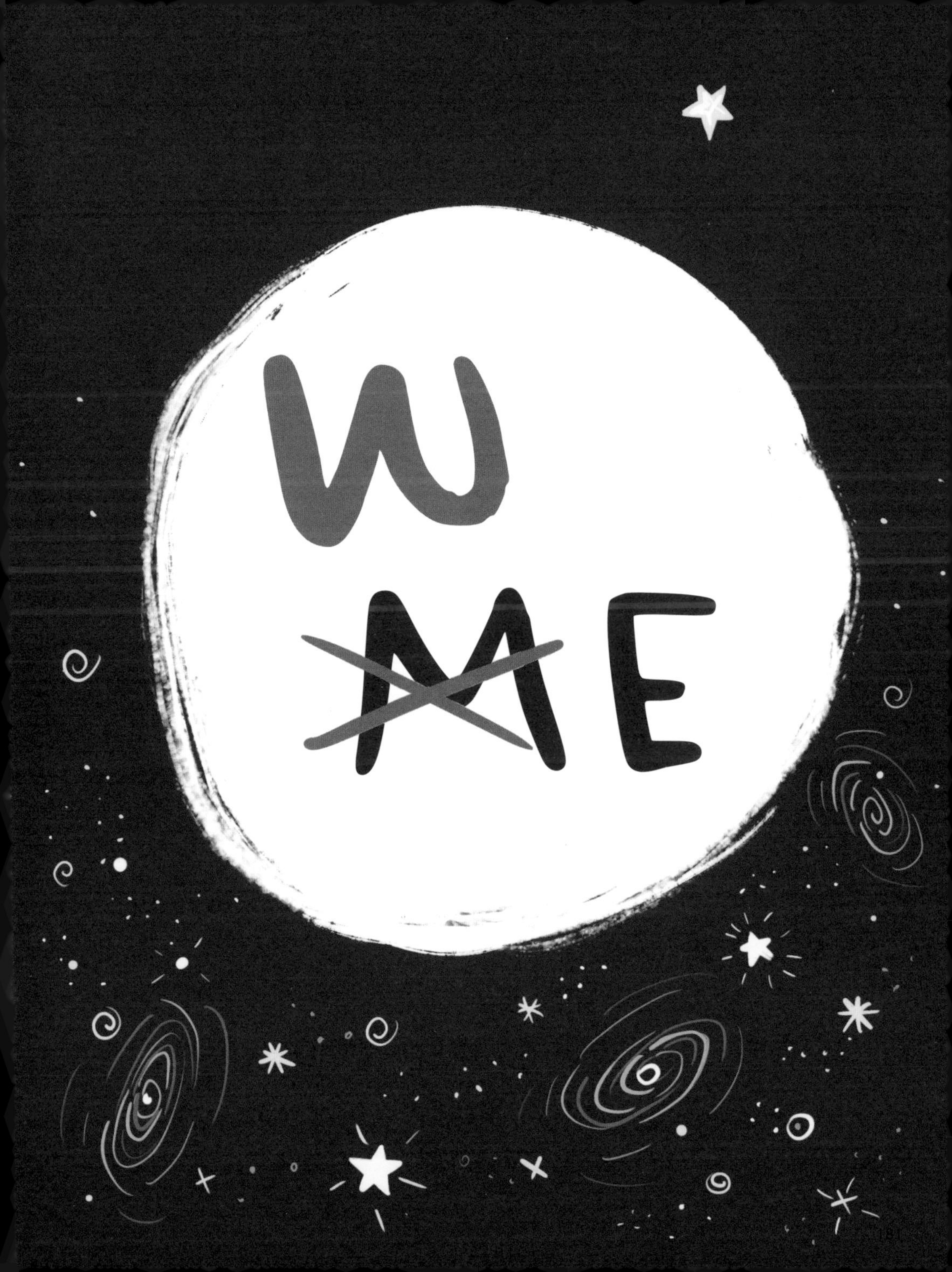
W
ME

Most of us want to feel a sense of belonging in our neighbourhoods. If we don't, we tend to assume it's just not 'that kind' of neighbourhood. Or maybe that our neighbours are somehow different from us and the people we normally mix with.

The thing is, though, community — just like hope — isn't usually something you magically stumble upon. It's something you create and participate in. And the magic of communities of place is that we can make connections with all sorts of people, not only those who reaffirm our opinions.

In 2017, the visionary Tessy Britton launched the Every One Every Day project to improve community connection in two boroughs of London. The transformation was remarkable. Mental and physical health in the boroughs improved. People became more engaged in local activities. Skills were shared. Community projects boomed. People even started voting more.

Other communities now look at Tessy's Participatory City Foundation as a way to improve their own social, environmental, economic and cultural standards.

So how do we build community? We engage in, support and start up community projects. The more projects there are, the more community there will be. Participation is contagious.

Why connect with community?

Mixing with others, no matter how similar or
different they seem, offers all sorts of benefits.

	SIMILAR	DIFFERENT
OPINIONS	Understanding & comfort	Discussion & learning
LIFESTYLE	Familiarity & compassion	New perspectives & insight

How to build connections where you live

INTRODUCE YOURSELF

Be authentically you.

Support local businesses and events. Introduce yourself. Remember names.

Learn about the history of where you live, including (especially) the indigenous history.

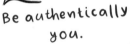

Speak about the things that matter to you.

Offer to share resources and/or produce.

$0

If you see someone who needs help, offer it.

If someone offers you help, accept it.

Go to meetings and learn about local issues.

Hidden friendships

Has this ever happened to you? There was someone you saw frequently. Maybe you sat next to them in class, on the bus or at the library.

You were friendly. You always said hello.

Maybe you did that awkward half smile, wide-eye thing.

But it never went further than a greeting.

Then one day, you saw them in one of 'your' places.
A place connected to your interests and hobbies, or to your
vision of a better future. A place where you didn't think
they would go (based on your own easy assumptions).

A connection was made, a common interest found.
A friendship was started — one that was there all along,
waiting to be unearthed,

if you'd been brave enough
to just start chatting.

Find YOUR people

Communities of interest provide spaces where you can geek out about the causes and hobbies you are passionate about. They can be face to face, online or even via the mail if you're the nostalgic type.

workshops and meet-ups

Social and support groups

Community projects ...

and drives

Special-interest events

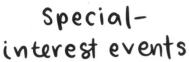

Religious & spiritual groups

Team sports

Book clubs

Political groups & causes

Local theatre and music groups

Communities as drivers of change

One of my best friends, Jacinta, is into sewing communities in a big way. She goes on sewing weekends, she teaches people to sew at the local community centre, she crochets, she knits, she quilts. Jacinta has many gifts but high at the top is the way she sprinkles everyone she meets with kindness and leaves them feeling more beautiful.

One day while we were hanging out, Jacinta reached into her handbag and pulled out a crochet hook and a small yellow circle. I looked at it and asked her what it was.

An online sewing community that she was involved in had recently uploaded a pattern and requested that each member crochet a daisy to be made into a blanket, to raise money for victim support. By the end of the campaign, they had received daisies from all over the world — far more than expected — and ended up with three blankets.

To sit down and crochet an entire blanket is a gigantic effort, a project that might feel too overwhelming to even start. But by dividing it up and allowing everyone to care for their own patch, the job got done. Hundreds of dainty daisies, connected into blankets made with nothing but wool and love.

This can be a helpful way to think about making change in the world.

I used to feel like one tiny piece of
an incredibly complex puzzle.

But the fact is, each of us is a tiny thread,
inextricably twisted together with other threads.

We're so much
stronger when we're
knitted together.

You can't make a community without 'U'!

On being an ally in your community (and beyond)

I am a middle-class, cisgendered, able-bodied white woman. For my entire life I have had access to health care and education, clean drinking water, ample nutrition and a warm bed. I have never been (directly) impacted by war, famine, terrorism or an authoritarian regime.

I have lived with Generalised Anxiety Disorder for most of my life, and I also have ADHD (which some people think stands for Attention Deficit and Hyperactivity Disorder, but to me means Amazingly, Daringly and Happily Different).

All this is to say that while I understand some discrimination, I don't understand it all. I have never feared for my life due to the colour of my skin, the religion I follow, or lack of access to resources or assistance. I can't educate on those things and I recommend that you look to people with those lived experiences to learn about them.

I can, however, share some of the lessons I have learned (or unlearned) along the way to trying to be an ally.

If it's not a better future for all, it's not a future worth fighting for. Own your privilege and show up for those who are denied theirs.

Look at your privilege

Having 'privilege' doesn't mean your life isn't hard. It means that it isn't harder for reasons beyond your control, such as the colour of your skin, your religious beliefs, your financial means, access to health care and so on.

Commit to lifelong learning ...

and UNlearning!

LISTEN to those with lived experience.

Whenever you learn about history, ask: whose point of view is this from? Whose point of view is missing?

Share the spotlight (AKA your visibility!)

walk through the world with an attitude of accessibility and inclusivity.

Stand alongside those with less privilege and, when needed, stand in front of them.

One person can
spark hope...

but a community can turn
hope into progress!

we've got this

Here we are at the end of the book and, hopefully,
at the beginning of a new way of seeing the future
we are marching towards.

Building a better future won't be a walk in the park
(unless maybe you're protesting?) but that's okay. As author
Glennon Doyle has famously said, 'We can do hard things.'

There's no getting around the fact that change is
uncomfortable — and we are always changing. Our bodies,
our lives, our world are constantly shifting, moment to
moment. That is the nature of life. The trick is to accept
that even though change can be uncomfortable, slow
and messy, it can also lead to something beautiful.

Remember in kindergarten when you learned about how a
squidgy, green sausage (a caterpillar) retreats to a chrysalis
only to emerge as a resplendent butterfly? So simple, so
poignant; however, what is rarely mentioned is what happens
inside the chrysalis. What does 'change' actually look like?

For a caterpillar to turn into a butterfly, it effectively dissolves into caterpillar soup. Yep, our triumphant bug-tube basically dissolves itself. It is an uncomfortable, ugly process — and caterpillars aren't the only ones who experience discomfort with change. Snakes become particularly aggressive while shedding their skin. Many species of birds retreat and get grumpy while moulting their feathers. And let's not get into what happens to adolescent humans as they go through puberty.

Change is hard. And, oh my, are we uncomfy right now.

Hope is looking at the bowl of caterpillar soup and understanding that somehow, inexplicably, almost impossibly, it has the potential to transform into a butterfly.

Hope is not the butterfly; hope is the caterpillar soup.

So, if things currently feel like 'soup' — how exciting! We have started on the way. The world may feel so terribly uncomfortable right now, the change may be slow, but it has begun. We've got this.

Support services

If you or someone you know is struggling to cope, there are mental health and crisis helplines staffed by people who know how to help. If your country's helpline is not listed below, visit worldhelplines.org for support near you. If you are under 18 years old, visit childhelplineinternational.org to find your local number.

Australia

If you or someone you know is in crisis, call 000 or go to the emergency room.

LIFELINE provides 24-hour crisis counselling, support groups and suicide prevention services. Call 13 11 14.

SANE AUSTRALIA offers support, training and education for those with a mental illness to lead a better life. Call 1800 187 263, 10 am–10 pm AEST (Mon–Fri).

QLIFE provides nationwide support for lesbian, gay, bisexual, transgender and intersex (LGBTIQ+) people of all ages. Call 1800 184 527, 3 pm–12 am AEST (7 days a week).

KIDS HELPLINE is Australia's only free 24/7 confidential and private counselling service for children and young people aged five to 25. Call 1800 55 1800.

New Zealand

If you or someone you know is in crisis, call 111 or go to the emergency room.

LIFELINE provides 24-hour crisis counselling, support groups and suicide prevention services. Call 0800 543 354 (0800 LIFELINE) or text 4357 (HELP) for free, 24/7 confidential support.

KIDSLINE offers free, confidential, 24/7 telephone support for children up to the age of 18. Call 0800 54 37 54 (0800 KIDSLINE).

SUICIDE CRISIS HELPLINE is a free, 24/7 nationwide service. Call 0508 828 865 (0508 TAUTOKO).

OUTLINE LGBTIQ+ HELPLINE is a free, confidential service. Call 0800 688 5463 (0800 OUTLINE), 6–9 pm (7 days a week).

United Kingdom

If you or someone you know is in crisis, call 999, go to the emergency room or search for your local crisis team.

SAMARITANS provides free, confidential, 24/7 emotional support for people experiencing despair, distress or suicidal thoughts. Call 116 123.

MIND provides free advice, support and information for people affected by mental health problems, as well as their family, friends and carers. Call 0300 123 3393 or text 86463, 9 am–6 pm (Mon–Fri, except bank holidays).

LGBT FOUNDATION offers phone support and advice for those struggling with mental health problems or loneliness, who want to report a hate crime or who need information on sexual health. Call 0345 3 30 30 30, 9 am–9 pm (Mon–Fri) and 10 am–6 pm (Sat–Sun).

CHILDLINE provides free, confidential, 24/7 emotional support for anyone under the age of 18 on issues including child abuse, neglect and bullying. Call 0800 1111.

United States of America

If you or someone you know is in crisis, call 911 or go to the emergency room.

NATIONAL SUICIDE PREVENTION LIFELINE is a national network of local crisis centres that provide free and confidential support 24/7. Call 1-800-273-8255.

SAMHSA NATIONAL HELPLINE provides trained crisis workers 24/7 who will listen to you and direct you to the mental health or substance abuse disorders resources you need. Call 1-800-662-4357 (or TTY 1-800-487-4889).

LGBT NATIONAL HOTLINE offers confidential one-to-one support, as well as local resources and information for cities and towns across the United States. Call 1-888-843-4564.

YOUR LIFE YOUR VOICE (Boys Town National Hotline) provides free, confidential, 24/7 support for kids, teens and young adults (both boys and girls) dealing with mental health problems, abuse, bullying, addiction, fighting with a parent or challenging circumstances. Call 1-800-448-3000.

Thank you

In his 1997 Lifetime Achievement Emmy award acceptance speech, one of my biggest heroes, Mister Rogers, said, 'So many people have helped me to come to this night. Some of you are here, some are far away, some are even in Heaven. All of us have special ones who have loved us into being.' So many people have loved me and this book into being.

To the incredible team at Murdoch Books — Jane, Julie, Megs, Melody and Carol — your support, knowledge and enthusiasm helped me make a dream come true. Especially my editor, Julie, who found me and my book as a little rock and then polished us into a gem. Mads: thank you for your design prowess on this absolute onion of a book (So. Many. Layers!) — you pulled the book together so beautifully.

To the people who have supported my work — the ones who have followed, shared, liked, bought or messaged kind words — your support means the world to me. Your passion, projects, dedication and thoughtful conversations are a big reason why I'm hopeful about the future.

To Mr Doria, Mrs Richards and Mrs Benwell: you are all teachers who may not know the impact you had on me by bolstering my self-belief and celebrating my 'lively' personality instead of trying to discipline it into submission. Mrs Richards, you probably don't even remember that on the last day of Year 7 you said you wanted a copy of my first book. I have carried that comment with me for the past 23 years and now you can expect a parcel in the post.

To all my friends and family who have cheered me on — Cint, Max, Dan, Tom, Claire, Candice, Garry, Bec, Uncle Mike and Aunty Trish. Some special mentions: Dino and Diana for your pragmatism, your listening ears and all the desserts. Sally O'Mally — my best friend who knows me better than I know myself. Jack and Bianca — you are two of the brightest sparks in my life (unless we're competing in a board game, in which case you can go to hell). Louise — I so badly wish you were here so we could clink a celebratory champagne glass together. My beautiful Bella — my adopted little sister — you make the world a better place.

To Mr Pug. I lost you while writing this book. I find myself listening for the click-click of your little feet following me around. You were the most loyal little man. I love and miss you, Monkey. Ally, your breath is the worst but your cuddles are the best. Joanie, your sass is inspiring.

Grandma, I wish we'd had more time, but I know you are looking down on me, cheering along as I follow in your footsteps. Thank you and Grandpa for raising such a strong, clever, loving daughter and then gifting her to me as my mum.

My Brother Bear, Tom, and my sissy, Terri, thank you for always swooping in whenever I need you — whether it's for loves in the hard times or laughs in the good times — and for giving my kids such wonderful cousins in John and Gia.

Mum and Dad. Mother Goose and Farsher. I don't know what cosmic lottery I won to get both of you as parents, but I do know that I'm thankful for it every day. There are not enough superlatives available to tell you how much your unwavering support and love means to me. So, I'll leave it at this:

you've always been my biggest fans and I hope you know that I am yours. I couldn't have done this without you . . . or Roley.

To my partner in crime, Mark: you have always believed in me (even when I haven't), been proud of my achievements and loved me for all my quirks. The past 14 years have been pretty damn great and now that we've finally chased our dreams and made the tree change, I'm excited to build a beautiful future with you. I love you millions and billions.

And finally . . . Lucy and Toby. My little wilds. You are both so wonderfully weird, bright, loving, curious, energetic, caring, adventurous and so damn funny. My life's work will be to help you stay as quirky as you are, because the world needs you exactly as you are. I love you more than anything else on this planet and I'm so proud to be your mum.

Published in 2021 by
Murdoch Books, an
imprint of Allen & Unwin

Murdoch Books Australia
83 Alexander Street
Crows Nest NSW 2065
Phone: +61 (0)2 8425 0100
murdochbooks.com.au
info@murdochbooks.com.au

Murdoch Books UK
Ormond House
26–27 Boswell Street
London WC1N 3JZ
Phone: +44 (0) 20 8785 5995
murdochbooks.co.uk
info@murdochbooks.co.uk

For corporate orders and
custom publishing, contact our
business development team at
salesenquiries@murdochbooks.
com.au

Publisher: Jane Morrow
Editorial Manager:
Julie Mazur Tribe
Design Manager: Megan Pigott
Designer: Madeleine Kane
Editor: Melody Lord
Production Director: Lou Playfair

Text and illustrations
© 2021 Emily Ehlers
The moral right of the author
has been asserted.
Design © 2021 Murdoch Books
Cover art © Emily Ehlers

ISBN 978 1 92235 134 0 Australia
ISBN 978 1 91166 817 6 UK

A catalogue record for this
book is available from the
National Library of Australia

A catalogue record for this
book is available from the
National Library of Australia

A catalogue record for this
book is available from the
British Library

Colour reproduction by
Splitting Image Colour Studio
Pty Ltd, Clayton, Victoria

Printed and bound in Singapore
by C.O.S. Printers Pte Ltd

10 9 8 7 6 5 4 3 2 1

References: page 50 Eric Weiner, *The Geography of Genius* (Simon & Schuster,
reprint 2016); page 64 Chimamanda Ngozi Adichie, TEDGlobal 2009, July 2009;
page 72 Joseph Campbell, *The Hero with a Thousand Faces* (Pantheon Books,
1949); page 90 Abraham Maslow (1943). 'A theory of human motivation',
Psychological Review 50 (4): 370–96. doi:10.1037/h0054346; page 118 Anita
Roddick, quoted in 'Anita The Agitator' by Philip Elmer-Dewitt, *TIME*, Sunday,
24 June, 2001; page 120 Stephen Covey, *The 7 Habits of Highly Effective People*
(Free Press, 1989); page 139 'Wind Beneath My Wings', Larry Henley and Jeff
Silbar, 1982; performed by Bette Midler, on *Beaches: Original Soundtrack
Recording*, Atlantic Records, 1989; page 182 Every One Every Day: Tessy Britton,
Founding Chief Executive, Participatory City Foundation, weareeveryone.org;
page 202 Glennon Doyle, *Untamed* (Random House, 2020).